123

of Australian Wildlife

Steve Parish

NATURE kids

EVERY KID'S A NATURE KID

D1401940

1 one

One dolphin dashing
across the water.

2 two

Two echidnas eating ants.

3 three

Three mice munching in the moonlight.

4 four

Four wombats wandering in the wild.

5 five

Five frilled lizards
frightening off foes.

6 six

Six sea stars
shimmering on
the sand.

7 seven

Seven turtle hatchlings heading for home.

8 eight

Eight scaly snakes
slithering sideways.

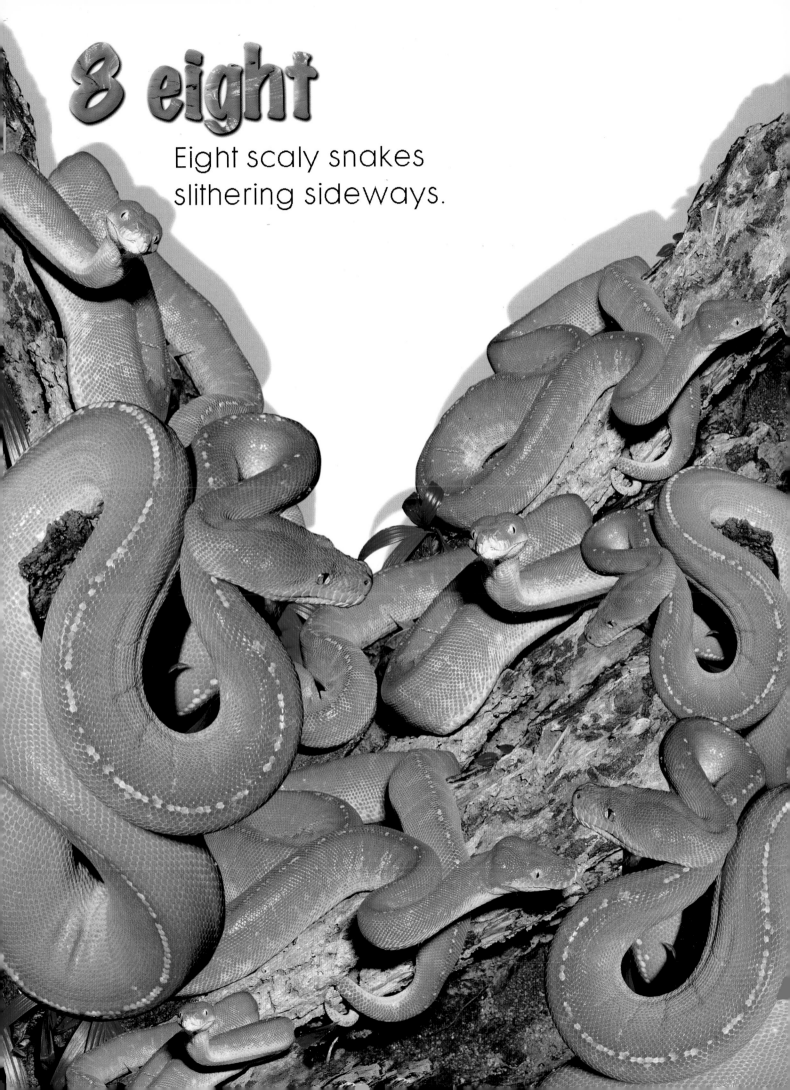

9 nine

Nine pelicans
preening
near a pool.

10 ten

Ten silver seagulls scrambling for scraps.

11 eleven

Eleven playful possums eating parts of plants.

12 twelve

Twelve koalas climbing
with others
of their kind.

13 thirteen

Thirteen clever cockatoos clustering in a crowd.

14 fourteen

Fourteen kangaroos gazing curiously at the camera.

15 fifteen

Fifteen bright bugs
bumbling backwards.

16 sixteen

Sixteen penguins parading peacefully.

17 seventeen

Seventeen frogs frolicking in the forest.

18 eighteen

Eighteen little lorikeets
landing lightly.

19 nineteen

Nineteen fish fluttering their fins.

20 twenty

Twenty brilliant butterflies bringing beauty to the bush.

1 one	11 eleven
2 two	12 twelve
3 three	13 thirteen
4 four	14 fourteen
5 five	15 fifteen
6 six	16 sixteen
7 seven	17 seventeen
8 eight	18 eighteen
9 nine	19 nineteen
10 ten	20 twenty